Bradford and its Trolleybuses

Preamble

This book is simply about Bradford's trolleybuses, at its largest numerically the fifth biggest fleet in the country, but anyone who has not visited Sandtoft, Dudley or Carlton Colville, where trolleybuses in preservation still operate, may well not be familiar with this type of transport, which disappeared from the streets of Britain over thirty years ago.

As Geoff Lumb's narrative explains, the trolleybus was a hybrid; neither a motorbus nor a heavy motor car. The former was subject to legislation under various Road Traffic Acts and overseen by the Ministry of Transport (as it was known in trolleybus days) and administered by the Regional Traffic Commissioners, both in respect of vehicle maintenance and services operated. The trolleybus owed its very existence in each location where it operated to a specific Act of Parliament; to drive one a separate driving test was required, which then became a category on one's normal driving licence (unlike the motorbus, where the licence to drive was issued by the Traffic Commissioner). The driver's hours regulations that applied to motorbuses did not apply to trolleybus work, but other regulatory measures under hackney carriage rules did apply, subject to the local government area in which the trolleybus operated.

Bradford and its Trolleybuses

Venture *publications*

Geoff Lumb

Cover: Bradford's ex-Darlington 71 seat (39 upstairs, 32 down) trolleybuses, rebodied to almost 29ft by East Lancashire, could carry only five standing and in the spring of 1960 the seating was reduced to 70 by removing a downstairs single seat. They could then carry eight standing passengers so increasing the maximum load by two. Number **788** is seen at Nab Wood on its way to Bingley in summer 1963. *(V Nutton courtesy G Lumb Collection)*

Rear Cover: The use of a single-deck ex-Darlington trolleybus allowed enthusiasts the opportunity to travel on a type of vehicle which had been previously used in Bradford from 1911 until late 1945. On 17th February 1957, No. **T403** was used for an enthusiasts' tour, and it is seen in Pasture Lane with one of the last completely new trolleybuses purchased by Bradford returning to the City from Pasture Lane. T403 was withdrawn from service at the end of January 1958 for rebodying. *(J Copland)*

Title page: Regular trolleybus services in Bradford ceased to operate on Friday, 24th March 1972. One of the nine trolleybuses in use during the day on the two remaining routes was No. **712**. It is seen in Thornton Road with two passengers experiencing travel by trolleybus for the last time. *(D J Smithies)*

Left: In early 1927, Railless Ltd, a major user of English Electric motors built at the Phoenix works in Bradford, ceased to manufacture trolleybuses. English Electric, concerned at this potential loss of work, stepped in to supply complete railless vehicles using a commercially available motorbus chassis modified to accommodate a traction motor and equipment. After use as a demonstrator the prototype trolleybus was converted from rear- to centre-entrance before being sold to Bradford, where it entered service in March 1929 as fleet number 560. After withdrawal from service in February 1939, single deck trolleybus No. **560** (**CK 3898**) was sold to a Mrs Dalby, who used it as a weekend holiday caravan at Dobrudden Farm, on the edge of Baildon Moor. When seen in January 1963 it had been unused for a number of years. *(G Lumb)*

No book about Bradford would be complete without reference to the large following of trolleybus enthusiasts who photographed the changing scene and made copious notes of new developments as they happened so many years ago. This book would have been the poorer without them. On 20th April 1952, the second annual tour of parts of the Bradford system was held using one of the twelve BUT 9611T trolleybuses supplied in 1949 with attractive 56-seat Roe bodies. This group photograph shows the enthusiasts posed in front of No. **748** (**EKU 748**). From the left: John Pitts, Eric Thornton, Bob Mack, Conductor and Driver (who was an inspector); crouching in front of 748, Raymond Addy and Arthur Brooke (Elland); to the right, front row: ?, John Taylor, boy behind David Packer, Eric Thornton's father, Colin Routh, ?, Donald Punchard, Mrs Ethel Hartley, Frank Hartley; back row, from left: Ralph Jackson, David Packer's father, Keith Flesher, Herbert Cheetham, Kenneth Mitchell, ?, Ian Smith, ?, Stanley King and John Humphrey. *(Roy Brook)*

Dedication

This book is dedicated to the memory of the Revd Chaceley T Humpidge, "The Apostle of the Trolleybus", who died on 30th June 1972. Mr Humpidge had a lifelong interest in trams and trolleybuses, and in the Church, which he entered after his retirement from Sheffield Transport in 1969.

Introduction

This is the first book in the Prestige Colour series to be devoted entirely to a single British trolleybus system. Bradford has the unique distinction of being the most longstanding trolleybus user, having operated them for over 61 years. Along with Leeds, they commenced operation on the same day in June 1911 and, when Bradford's system finally closed on 26th March 1972, it was the last survivor of the fifty municipalities or companies in this country who had used this efficient, economical and silent form of transport for its citizens. This achievement was only possible through the inspiration, innovation, dedication, dogged determination and prudent use of financial resources by the managers, loyally supported by council committees.

Each of the periods 1911-8, 1918-30 or 1931-40, when C J Spencer, R H Wilkinson and C R Tattam were respectively developing the system, could be termed "The Heyday of the Bradford Trolleybus". By February 1951, when C T Humpidge became manager, the system could perhaps have been described as marking time. "Make do and mend" policies had been pursued throughout the previous decade during the wartime and subsequent postwar shortages, which had not necessarily been the case with some other systems. Furthermore, rising operating costs, outstripping those of the motorbus, coupled with the removal of the incentive to use electrical power after nationalisation of the Bradford municipal electric supply department, was leading Bradford Corporation Passenger Transport Committee to question the continued operation of the "trackless". It should be remembered that at the time it was in the throes of closing the remains of the tramway system. The committee even tried to cancel its 1949 order for eight BUT trolleybuses with Weymann bodies.

Chaceley Humpidge was undoubtedly an enthusiast for electric traction: but he was also a realist. Fashion often dictates progress and it was certainly fashionable by 1951 to replace worn-out trams with motorbuses, and even Birmingham, his home city, had replaced its 74-strong trolleybus fleet with motorbuses in July 1951, in the interests of standardisation. Yet Humpidge saw a way of retaining and expanding the system without incurring crippling capital outlays.

The City Fathers were not against trolleybuses as such, but they had to consider the ratepayers and the costs involved. There had to be a reasonable return on capital, at a time when motorbuses were becoming comparatively cheaper both in capital outlay and operating costs: new trolleybuses and their infrastructure were not really viable. Humpidge knew that there was a way round the problem. The City was no stranger to ways of extending the life of its vehicles by rebodying: why not rebody second-hand vehicles, thus halving the capital cost of providing "new" vehicles? The availability of cast-offs from other systems meant that Bradford could have its pick. In many cases there was not even the need to rebody.

The true costs of rebodying - more than some might think - were still less than the price of brand new vehicles. If chassis were bought for spares they could conceivably be purchased from the revenue account as operating costs and probably did not need to be referred to the Finance Committee and Whitehall. The availability of the large workforce employed at Thornbury Works, to undertake major work on rebuilding chassis, allowed much to be done in house, with true costs lost as part of the general overhead.

The use of elderly chassis and parts in rebuilding exercises meant that many technical innovations and design improvements, introduced by manufacturers on new chassis to reduce maintenance costs, did not pertain in Bradford, which was thus limited in how far it could go in moving with the times. Since the trolleybus was a hybrid vehicle, which was legally neither a light locomotive nor a motorcar under the various acts governing road vehicles, there were sometimes difficulties if an offence was committed under the Road Traffic Acts - how did one prosecute? It also meant that trolleybuses were not, as were motorbuses, subject to periodic recertification, and while the life expectancy of trolleybuses was always intended to be longer than that of a comparable motorbus, as a result they could run higher mileages between overhauls - yet often identical components were subject to the same rate of wear in both types of vehicle. Although driver error was undoubtedly a significant factor in some instances, that high mileage between overhauls may explain why more trolleybuses overturned than did motorbuses on Bradford's roads. Other systems with identical vehicles did not seem to encounter this problem.

That is the background to the Indian Summer made possible by the skilful management of the undertaking between 1951 and 1961 by Chaceley Humpidge, who made it possible for the system to survive until 1972, when the last two routes were withdrawn. It was under the management of John C Wake, who succeeded Humpidge in July 1961 but left in November 1962 to become General Manager of Nottingham City Transport, that the decline of the Bradford trolleybus started. Final dismemberment of the system was left to Edward Deakin, General Manager from 1962, who - almost reluctantly - presided over the gradual run-down to final closure with normal service ceasing on 24th March 1972.

My first visit to see Bradford trolleybuses was in July 1951 when I travelled to Thornbury on unrebuilt Jo'burg 693, returning from Bradford Moor on 745. In February 1952, at half-term, friends and I travelled from Crossflatts to Bradford Moor, as part of a circular tour around the present West Yorkshire. After receiving an inexpensive 120 camera for Christmas 1952, Bradford trolleybuses 608 and 598 - AEC/EE with NCB MK I and II bodies - were subjects on my second film and were my first trolleybus pictures.

This homage to Bradford and its trolleybuses uses colour material covering the period 1950 to 1972 and portrays many of the variations in liveries and chassis/body combinations that could be seen during those last 22 years. The author has chosen to place them in chronological order of age of body or date of acquisition from 1951, and hopes readers enjoy this glimpse of a form of transport which disappeared from the streets of Bradford 31 years ago.

Acknowledgements

I would like to thank the following for allowing me access to their photographic collections : Roy Brook, C Carter, J Copland, V Nutton, D J Smithies, A Thornton and G Warnes. The following people were consulted to ensure that the introduction and captions were not too badly affected by the "rose coloured spectacles" syndrome: Philip Jenkinson, Mick Leak and David J Smithies. Bob Rowe, John Senior and John Banks have also worked on the text to its great benefit. Finally, grateful thanks to my wife, Ethel, for translating scribbled notes into legible captions on disk and to Ann Williams for converting that into the required format. Without their help this interpretation of Britain's first and last trolleybus system would not have been possible.

Geoff Lumb
Huddersfield
February 2003.

Above: The body from an even earlier trolleybus than that shown on page 2, Railless Electric Vehicle (REV) No. **515**, built by Bradford Corporation in 1914, was recovered in October 1973 from an allotment at Tong for a long-term preservation project. It is shown in store in Huddersfield in August 1975, and is now in store in the Bradford Industrial Museum. Number 515 was one of 17 REVs placed into service between June 1914 and April 1915. The REV was designed by the Bradford Manager, C J Spencer and the Tramways Engineer, J W Dawson. The chassis was assembled by David Brown & Sons Ltd, of Huddersfield. *(G Lumb)*

Above and right: English Electric built 93 trolleybuses between July 1928 and August 1931 using traction equipment supplied by Phoenix Works, Bradford. Fifty-three of these were purchased by Bradford, with the last examples remaining in service until 1946. After withdrawal, one of the single-deck examples, No. **562**, was sold by a Leeds dealer for use as a caravan at Eastoft, then in the West Riding of Yorkshire. When no longer required as a caravan, it remained on site from 1973 until 1989, when the son of the family who had used it, who was now an influential businessman, moved it into store at his Elland premises in 2001. This, the only known survivor of those 93 English Electric Phoenix Works-built trolleybuses and a rare example of an early British trolleybus, built when speed limits were just 20mph, was moved to the Trolleybus Museum at Sandtoft, where in due course it will be restored to its original splendour. *(G Lumb Collection; B Maguire)*

>> **Opposite page:** The earliest colour views of Bradford trolleybuses located by the author date from 1950. During the Second World War, one of the Ministry of Transport directives was that public service vehicles serving factories involved in war work should be camouflaged to escape detection from the air. Accordingly, Bradford painted most of its motorbuses, when due for repainting, into an all-over khaki livery. Trolleybuses not subject to the same legislation were painted into a brighter livery from mid-1942, the earlier ultramarine and cream being replaced by "Bradford Blue" and "broken white" - the broken white was actually primrose. The earlier grey roofs, with black beading, mudguards and fenders, and gold transfers were retained, although lining-out was changed from gold to yellow. This view of No. **671** shows this livery, which included legal lettering on the offside as well as the nearside. This vehicle was one of the 42 AEC/EE trolleybuses purchased in 1938/9. It was photographed in front of the fire-damaged YMCA building in Forster Square: the aftermath of the fire disrupted services through Forster Square in June and July 1950. *(C Carter)*

Above: Number **647**, another of the 42 AEC/EE 661T trolleybuses, Nos 635-76 (CAK 635-76) introduced in 1938/9, is seen in 1950 in Thornton Road waiting to depart to Pasture Lane as a "duplicate bus". Regular short workings did not commence until 25th February 1951, when most of the Lidget Green shorts were extended to serve Pasture Lane. *(C Carter)*

>> **Opposite page:** This view of Thornton Road showing the Clayton stand was taken in June 1955 and shows that passengers had been provided with a shelter. By this time the livery had changed again - with no lining out or grey roof and the loss of the two white bands below the windows. The lack of traffic suggests that this photograph was taken on a Sunday afternoon - the clock shows that it was 4.30pm. *(J Copland)*

Above: Number **639** is seen at Five Lane Ends in April 1954, returning to the City from Greengates on route 42. The wiring at this junction was altered in 1957 to include a full circle, enabling vehicles to proceed on any of the three roads at this junction. In order to achieve financial savings, the practice of lining out had ceased in late 1950, and from 1951 painting the primrose bands was discontinued. After June 1953 further simplification was achieved with roofs being painted blue instead of grey. *(J Copland)*

>> *Opposite page:* In 1938, Bradford ordered 57 trolleybuses from English Electric Co Ltd. As already mentioned, 42 were EEC-bodied AEC/EE type 661T vehicles. The other 15 were subcontracted by EEC to Karrier Motors Ltd who supplied its E4 model with EE equipment. The bodies were built by Weymann. These 15 became 677-91 (CAK 677-91). At this time, two directors of AEC were also on the board of Sunbeam Commercial Vehicles Ltd, who built both Karrier and Sunbeam trolleybuses in the same factory at

Moorfields, Wolverhampton. SCV used AEC axles when building its trolleybuses. It was also a major supplier of components to AEC for their vehicles. Number **690**, one of the Karriers, is seen in June 1955 climbing Little Horton Lane on its way to Wibsey. These vehicles displayed a combined English Electric-Karrier winged motif on the front dash. 690 was withdrawn in December 1955. *(J Copland)*

Above: During 1940, Bradford was able to borrow four AEC trolleybuses from Southend-on-Sea Corporation, an event that inspired the change in livery in 1942. After they had been returned in February 1942, Bradford was able to obtain ten of the 25 Sunbeam MF2 trolleybuses which could not be shipped to the South African city of Johannesburg. These vehicles, which were 8ft wide, arrived between June and October 1942,

enabling Bradford to withdraw nine of the 1934 AEC trolleybuses and replace the life-expired English Electric bodies with 58-seat utility bodies built by Brush at Loughborough. One of these, No. **606**, is seen outside Duckworth Lane Depot in September 1953. Note the unusual position of the rear fleet number. Wimsol was a popular household cleaning fluid of the day in the battle between Procter & Gamble and Lever Bros,

probably now long forgotten, whereas Tizer and Bovril are still popular products. *(J Copland)*

>> *Opposite page:* Number **612**, one of the two trolleybuses used on the annual tour in 1956, was another of the nine to be rebodied by Brush in 1944. It is seen on 16th September turning from Toller Lane into Little Lane, which allowed access to Duckworth Lane depot from the City. *(J Copland)*

LITTLE HORTOI

SIGN OF SOUND VALUE ⬢CWS AT YOUR CO-OPERATIVE STORE

612

KY 8215

Above: At the bottom of Little Lane, No. **612** had turned left before stopping outside Duckworth Lane depot. Seen outside the depot is sister vehicle **601** and one of the ten Sunbeam MF2 trolleybuses (fleet Nos 693-702) diverted to Bradford in 1942. They had been fitted with Weymann utility bodies and because they were 8ft wide could work only designated routes, until 1950. In 1952/3 they were all withdrawn from service because of the condition of their bodies. After refurbishment, they received new East Lancashire Coachbuilders bodies and all of them returned to service in January 1956. Number **701** is seen with its experimental sliding platform doors which it retained until 1962. *(Roy Brook)*

>> *Opposite page:* In June 1957, another of the nine Brush-rebodied AEC/EE trolleybuses, No. **605**, is seen climbing up Little Horton Lane on the way to St Enoch's Road Top. Following it *en route* from Bradford's Chester Street bus station is one of the Hebble Motor Services AEC Regent III motorbuses fitted with a Roe 53-seat lowbridge body. Number **28 (AJX 243)** was one of six new in December 1948. *(J Copland)*

Above: In September 1957, another of the Brush-rebodied AEC/EE trolleybuses, No. **600**, climbs through Allerton village. When this route was converted from tramway operation many of the tramway poles and bracket arms were retained. This meant that the outward wires were on the wrong side of the road, well shown in this rural scene at the edge of the Yorkshire Moors. *(J Copland)*

>> *Opposite page:* Bradford had to wait until 1945 for its next Ministry of War Transport allocation of new vehicles which arrived between May and August 1945. Number **704**, one of twelve Karrier W4 trolleybuses, Nos 703-14 (DKY 703-14), fitted with Roe 56-seat utility bodies, is seen in May 1955, passing Peel Park, Bolton Road on its way back from Eccleshill Mechanics Institute. *(J Copland)*

When the MoWT allocated the ten Sunbeam MF2 trolleybuses in 1942, they displaced ten of the 1929-31 English Electric-built three-axle trolleybuses, which Bradford was instructed to sell to Newcastle Corporation. In 1945, a further three were sold to South Shields Corporation, who in 1942 had purchased the only AEC Q-type trolleybus operated at Bradford.

Above: In May 1959 one of the 1945 Roe utility-bodied trolleybuses on Karrier W4 chassis is seen outside Thornbury Depot. *(G Warnes)*

>> *Opposite page:* The next batch of Ministry of War Transport-allocated trolleybuses entered service in November 1945 to May 1946. This time the 19 Karrier W4 chassis were fitted with Park Royal 56-seat utility bodies; they carried fleet numbers 715-33 with registrations DKY 715-33. Number **728** is seen in Highfield Road in July 1955 returning from Saltaire to the City on route 40. *(J Copland)*

The placing into service in 1945/6 of 37 Karrier W4 trolleybuses allowed Bradford to withdraw all the remaining pre-1934 vehicles, comprising the last ten single-deck and the remaining twelve three-axle trolleybuses

Above: The final batch of MoWT-allocated trolleybuses was placed in service in April/May 1946 and comprised six Karrier W4 chassis with similar Roe bodies to those on 703-14, although sliding ventilators were fitted instead of drop windows. They carried fleet Nos. 734-9, again with matching DKY registrations. In March 1954, No. **737** is seen at the Greengates terminus in an atmospheric photograph that includes the corner shop and gasholder; the lack of TV aerials is a reminder that at that time evening travel for entertainment was the norm for most, and only a few had a television at home. *(J Copland)*

>> *Opposite page:* The influx of new trolleybuses in 1945/6 enabled a further six of the AEC/EE 661T trolleybuses to be rebodied with 56-seat Northern Coach Builders bodies built in Newcastle, the six being 607, 614-6, with KY registrations, new in 1934, and 621/2, 1935 examples with AAK registrations. Number **621** is seen in Killinghall Road, Undercliffe, in July 1955 on its way from Bolton Junction to Bankfoot, a through route introduced in October 1914. The section from Laisterdyke to Dudley Hill was the original 24th June 1911 route which had been ceremonially opened on 20th June. *(J Copland)*

21

Above: In August 1960, No. **622**, one of the six NCB Mark I-rebodied trolleybuses, is seen negotiating Forster Square on its way to Saltaire. *(V Nutton courtesy G Lumb Collection)*

>> ***Opposite page:*** Between October 1947 and December 1950, a further 21 of the original 1934/5 AEC/EE type 661T trolleybuses were rebodied with 56-seat Northern Coach Builders bodies. These were to an improved design and were identified as Mark II bodies. Number **629** re-entered service after rebodying in October 1947 and is seen at The Avenue, Clayton, in September 1956. The Clayton route 37 had been extended three quarters of a mile from Town End along The Avenue on 15th July 1956, which then became the terminus until 30th May 1970 when the route was cut back to Town End. *(J Copland)*

Above: One of the Mark II NCB-bodied AEC/EE trolleybuses, No. **603** (**KY 8206**), was repainted in the 1911 style of livery for the Trolleybus Golden Jubilee in June 1961. It is seen on the special tour for enthusiasts organised on 24th June 1961. It has just reversed into Dorchester Crescent from Knowles Lane using the reversing triangle at Holme Wood terminus. The gentleman on the left, clutching his cine camera, is the well known author, historian and photographer, Roy Brook.

Number 603 completed its one millionth mile in April 1962. It was withdrawn from service at the end of June 1962 - not bad for a vehicle new in November 1934. *(G Lumb)*

>> ***Opposite page:*** Bradford's first new postwar trolleybuses, Nos 740-51 (EKU 740-51), comprised attractive 8ft-wide Roe bodies mounted on BUT type 9611T chassis which introduced 120 horse-power vehicles to the fleet; No. 740 entered service in May 1949 and the rest

followed in December. At that time the only 8ft-wide trolleybuses in Bradford were the ten Johannesburgs diverted to the fleet in 1942. Until 1950, 8ft-wide vehicles could be operated only on designated routes approved by the Ministry of Transport and 740-51 went to Saltaire to work the Crossflatts route. Number **751** is seen in September 1954, the driver's hand signal indicating that he is pulling away from the kerb at Lister Park. *(J Copland)*

Above: Only two miles of the seven-mile route to Crossflatts was within the city. The depot at Saltaire was located within the boundaries of Shipley UDC, which allowed Bradford to provide services. From Nab Wood to Crossflatts the route was in the area of Bingley UDC which, until the end of trolleybus operation on 31st October 1963, issued annual licences for each trolleybus permitted to operate in their area. The licence specified that the vehicle should display a plate identifying its licence number. This view of Saltaire depot in September 1962 shows two of the Crossflatts trolleybuses, **744** and **746** (Bingley licence No. 42) as well as **799** which was in use on the Saltaire - Thackley - City route 40. The Keighley-West Yorkshire bus, **KDB57** (**HWW 884**), a Bristol K6B with ECW 55-seat lowbridge body, new in 1950, is waiting time before continuing to Leeds. *(J Copland)*

>> *Opposite page:* At the end of February 1964, No. **749**, one of the twelve 1949 BUT 9611T trolleybuses, was withdrawn from service and stored for four years before being put back into service on 21st March 1968. On 15th April 1968, it was used on an enthusiasts' tour over various remaining routes. It is seen at Thackley Corner returning to the City from Saltaire. The state of 749, with rusty front wings, is a reminder that trolleybuses were not subject to the examination by certifying officers that was mandatory for all motorbuses over seven years old. Hence in many cases maintenance of trolleybuses was not to the same standards, since the provisions of the 1930 Road Traffic Act did not apply. One example of different provisions was that trolleybuses required a daily earth-leakage test to ensure that passengers were in no danger of receiving an electric shock. *(J Copland)*

Above: Four of the twelve BUT trolleybuses with Roe bodies survived until 1970/1. Number **749** was the first of these four to be withdrawn: it succumbed on 3rd June 1970 after a collision with a bus. It is seen at Town End, Clayton, on 31st May 1970 with the driver having placed the chock under the offside-front wheel, to prevent an early, driverless departure backwards. On 1st June 1970, 749 was also the first trolleybus to use the Town End, Clayton, terminus after the route was cut back from The Avenue. *(J Copland)*

>> *Opposite page:* Numerically the first AEC/EE type 661T trolleybus in the Bradford fleet, 1934 No. 597 was rebodied with an NCB Mk II body in July 1948. After withdrawal from service in July 1962 it was transferred to the driver-training school and renumbered **060**. In June 1964 it was retired and replaced by BUT No. 745. When seen in March 1964, 060 was on training duties using the turning circle at Bell Dean Road, on the Thornton route; this turning circle was dismantled in May 1965. Bradford was unusual in having bespoke off-road training facilities; these were situated at Bowling. It also possessed a dual-control vehicle for in-house training of its drivers, as illustrated on page 30. *(J Copland)*

<< *Opposite page:* Another trolleybus-driver training vehicle was BUT No. 743, which was numbered **062** from December 1966; in December 1970 it was purchased for preservation by the National Trolleybus Association. It has since changed ownership and is now at the Sandtoft Trolleybus Museum, where it will be restored as a dual-control driver-trainer. It is seen outside Duckworth Lane Depot in May 1967. Compare the background with the photograph on page 12. *(J Copland)*

Above: During 1950 four of the 15 Karrier E4 trolleybuses new in 1938/9 had their Weymann bodies rebuilt by Samlesbury Engineering, of Samlesbury, near Preston. The major change in appearance was the replacement of the half-drop windows by sliding ventilators. Number **679** is seen in September 1953 at the Greengates terminus of route 42. The background provides a fine example of the age of steam in industry. 679 was withdrawn in 1960. *(J Copland)*

Above: In 1961 No. **687**, one of the four rebuilt Karrier E4 trolleybuses, was repainted into the 1939 ultramarine and cream livery to celebrate the Golden Jubilee of Bradford trolleybuses. On Saturday 24th June 1961, it and other vehicles were used to work a tour for enthusiasts, and after visiting a special exhibition in Lister Park, 687 used the Frizinghall turning circle at the bottom of Ashfield Avenue. This view shows the problems when drivers not accustomed to turning here misjudged it, and had to shunt back and forward until enough room was available to avoid going over the pavement. Many of Bradford's turning points did not allow for parked vehicles or for traffic, which was becoming denser. Number 687 was withdrawn in November 1962. *(G Lumb)*

>> *Opposite page:* Bradford's last completely new trolleybuses entered service in January 1951. This time the BUT 9611T chassis were fitted with Weymann 56-seat bodies, again 8ft wide. In January 1955, No. **754** is seen at Chelmsford Road en route to Saltaire from Bradford Moor. The turning circle for short working to Chelmsford Road had not been used that day. *(J Copland)*

Left: Seen loading in Forster Square in 1961 *en route* to Bradford Moor is 1951 BUT No. **757**. These BUTs became regular performers on the cross-city service to Crossflatts. *(Roy Brook)*

>> *Opposite page:* By 1929 the administration offices of Bradford Corporation were housed at 11 Forster Square, which was an ideal vantage point for the manager to observe many of the services passing through the square. The author, whilst one of the enthusiast guests at the Bradford Trolleybus Jubilee Dinner held there on Saturday 24th June 1961, was able to take this view of Forster Square which shows the differences in the treatment of the roofs on the 1950 Roe-bodied and the 1951 Weymann-bodied BUT type 9611T trolleybuses. *(G Lumb)*

Left: In March 1952, 13 trolleybuses returned to service after being fitted with new bodies, this time built by Crossley Motors Ltd, of Stockport. The 56-seat bodies were fitted to five AEC/EE type 661T and eight Karrier type E4 refurbished chassis, which had all been built in 1938-40. In July 1963 one of the rebodied Karriers, No. **678**, is seen negotiating the junctions outside Thornbury depot on its way back to the City. This vehicle was the first in the fleet to have matching fleet and registration numbers. *(G Lumb)*

Below: Number **640**, one of the five Crossley-rebodied AEC/EE type 661T trolleybuses, rebodied in 1952, is seen with the driver and conductress enjoying a breather at Thornbury terminus in July 1963. The conductress is carrying one of the five-value Bell Punch "Ultimate" ticket machines introduced in 1950. *(G Lumb)*

<< *Opposite page:* This 1961 view shows the curve, added in August 1960, linking Leeds Old Road to Killinghall Road at Barrack Tavern, which allowed trolleybuses to be road tested around the "depot circuit" from Thornbury depot via Bradford Moor, Barrack Tavern, Laisterdyke and back to the depot; the circuit remained in use until 25th March 1972. BUT No. **757** is seen going to Crossflatts using wiring which became redundant on 17th November 1962. The wiring from left to right in the picture was part of the Bolton to Bankfoot route inaugurated in 1914, and which operated for the last time on 29th February 1964. Arrangements for feeding the overhead line may be seen clearly; 757 is about to pass under the negative feed, and the positive feed (to the line continuing to Bankfoot) may be seen at the top of the picture. *(G Lumb)*

<< **Opposite page:** When Chaceley Thornton Humpidge, B.Sc. (C.Eng.), M.Inst.T., was appointed General Manager at Bradford in February 1951, it was the beginning of ten years of improvements to the trolleybus system. The first new route as part of the Humpidge programme, the 45 to Wibsey, with short route workings numbered 44 to St Enoch's Road Top, were operated by trolleybuses from the morning of Sunday 24th April 1955. The first one to turn at St Enoch's Road Top was **685**, one of the rebodied Karriers. On 8th April 1956, an extension was built from the 44 terminus into the Buttershaw estate. The driver has overshot and his vehicle is standing in a dead section of the overhead. He doubtless knows that the gradient will allow him to coast away without problem but situations like this required the drivers to be familiar with the overhead layout. *(J Copland)*

Above: The last Karrier E4 trolleybus to be built was acquired by Bradford, entering service in January 1940 as fleet No. **692**. It is believed that it was built as an exhibit for display at the Commercial Motor Show planned for November 1939, which was cancelled on the outbreak of the Second World War on 3rd September. Like the 15 earlier Karriers, it had a Weymann body and was the only trolleybus to carry a DKU registration. It was also one of the eight Karrier E4s to be rebodied by Crossley. It is seen in August 1962 in Allerton Road, having turned round at Chapel Lane to return to the City, with an incorrect blind display. *(J Copland)*

Above: In September 1952, Bradford purchased the entire fleet of 32 trolleybuses about to be withdrawn by the Nottinghamshire and Derbyshire Traction Company Ltd. By the time Notts & Derby closed on 25th April 1953, Bradford had already taken delivery of nine vehicles. Number 774, one of the 1949 BUT 9611T vehicles, was the first to enter service on 22nd April 1953, in Notts & Derby blue, with No. **596** following on 8th May already in full Bradford livery with a grey roof, having been painted by Notts & Derby before despatch to Bradford. It is seen at Allerton in September 1954. See page 48 for further details. *(J Copland)*

>> *Opposite page:* To commemorate the Coronation of HM Queen Elizabeth II on 2nd June 1953, two of the Notts & Derby BUT trolleybuses entered service painted in a special light blue and cream livery. Number **764 (NNU 228)** is seen at Thornbury on 26th September 1953. *(J Copland)*

Above: Number **769** (**NNU 233**), the second Coronation special, is seen near the Arcadian Cinema on the Clayton route on 5th September 1953. Note the variation in style of painting on the two Coronation trolleybuses. Two motorbuses were similarly treated. The 15 Notts & Derby BUT trolleybuses carried Weymann 56-seat bodies but, unlike Bradford's 752-9, were only 7ft 6ins wide. *(J Copland)*

>> *Opposite page:* The arrival of 15 second-hand 1949 BUT type 9611T trolleybuses in first-class condition, painted in a darker blue livery, enabled Bradford to place many of them into service without repainting. This view taken on 1st August 1954 outside Thornbury Depot shows No. **677**, one of the Karriers rebodied in March 1952, with a grey roof; BUT No. **770**, still in Notts & Derby blue; and No. **645**, one of the 1938 AEC/EE 661T trolleybuses still with its original body. *(J Copland)*

43

Above: Impressed with the simpler Notts & Derby livery, which used blue, white and black, Bradford started in June 1953 to repaint all vehicles with blue roofs instead of grey, in an effort to keep costs under control. This view taken on 11th July 1954 shows ex-Notts & Derby BUT No. **765** (**NNU 229**) resplendent in this simpler style of painting. It is seen at the Rooley Lane terminus at Bankfoot waiting to depart to Bolton.

Trolleybuses had waited here since 1914 and would do until 1964: was there another terminus anywhere in the country which remained unchanged for 50 years? Two weeks later, on 25th July, the frequency on this route was considerably reduced when the City Circle motorbus service commenced. As a further economy measure the trolleybus service was withdrawn on 29th February 1964. *(J Copland)*

>> *Opposite page:* The Notts & Derby trolleybuses were placed into service with their original destination boxes suitably over-painted to give a "number over terminus" display at the front and a number blind at the rear. Number 772 was fitted with standard-layout blinds in 1953 and No. **760** (**NNU 224**) was one of the further six to be so treated in 1959/60. It is seen outside Thornbury Depot in September 1962. *(G Lumb)*

Above: Number **587**, one of the ten 1941/2 Notts & Derby AEC/EE type 661T trolleybuses (Bradford Nos 587-96) is seen in Sunbridge Road in March 1955 loading for Duckworth Lane. Its Weymann body seated 56. The number of pedestrians suggests that the picture was taken during a busy time of the day but the absence of motor vehicles is remarkable. *(J Copland)*

>> *Opposite page:* Ex-Notts & Derby No. **588** started its Bradford service in its former owner's blue and is seen at the original 1935/6 Duckworth Lane terminus in Little Lane. The driver, having left the cab, has placed a chock on a chain in front of the offside-front wheel. *(J A Pitts via J Copland Collection)*

Above: The seven oldest vehicles purchased from Notts & Derby were 56-seat Weymann-bodied AEC/EE type 661T trolleybuses which became Bradford 580-6 (DRB 616-22). These 1937-built vehicles entered service between October 1954 and June 1955. Like those on the other ex-Notts & Derby trolleybuses, the Weymann bodies incorporated the MCW-patented trolley gantry within the double skin of the roof. Number **580**, originally Notts & Derby 300, is seen at Allerton in September 1957. This batch of seven were used as float vehicles enabling newer vehicles to be taken out of service for rebodying and remained in service only until 1958. *(J Copland)*

>> *Opposite page:* After the agreement in September 1952 to purchase the Notts & Derby fleet, Bradford then, in January 1953, purchased ten of the twelve Karrier W4 trolleybuses withdrawn in November 1952 on the closure of the Llanelly system operated by South Wales Transport, this time taking delivery of the chassis only for eventual rebodying. In order to provide stocks of spares for these rebodied vehicles, in September/October 1954 a further ten Karrier single-deck trolleybuses arrived from Darlington. Eight were dismantled but two, GHN 403/4, were given fleet numbers T403 and T404 and were tested over parts of the system after being overhauled. **T404** is seen outside the Thornbury Works in March 1955. Unlike its brother, T405, this one never entered passenger service. The Construction & Use Regulations at that time allowed double deck vehicles to be not more than 27ft long, hence the longer single-deck chassis were at that time of no use for rebodying as double-deckers. *(J Copland)*

Above: While the first of the 30 trolleybus chassis were at East Lancashire Coachbuilders being fitted with new bodies, Bradford's then assistant rolling stock engineer, J R Hanchett, removed one of the 1947 Northern Coach Builders Mark II bodies from 1935 AEC/EE trolleybus 618 and refitted it on to 639, a similar chassis, but three years newer. Number **639** returned to service in February 1956 and is seen with its second-hand body waiting to leave Hall Ings for Thornbury in May 1956. *(J Copland)*

>> Opposite page: The 30 rebodied trolleybuses used the chassis from the ten Johannesburg Sunbeam MF2s new in 1942, the ten ex-Llanelly Karrier W4 chassis and ten of Bradford's 1938/9 AEC/EE 661T chassis. All were rebuilt with 8ft-wide bodywork and were the first 27ft-long bodies in the trolleybus fleet. One of the Johannesburg Sunbeams, No. **695** (**DKW 995**), is seen in August 1962 in Union Street, the terminus of the Holme Wood service and the last new extension, introduced in March 1960. These ten all returned to service in January 1956. *(G Lumb)*

One of the ten Llanelly Karrier type W4 rebodied chassis, No. **777**, is seen parked at the Pasture Lane railway bridge whilst being used for the annual tour in September 1956. One of the earlier NCB-rebodied AEC/EE trolleybuses can be seen in the background on short workings to Pasture Lane. The ten Llanelly chassis had been modified to take the 8ft-wide bodies and all returned to service in February and March 1956. *(Roy Brook)*

Above: The ten rebodied AEC trolleybus chassis were modified to take the 8ft-wide bodies, including No. **634**, the only BAK-registered vehicle. When new it had been displayed on the English Electric stand at the November 1937 Commercial Motor Show, English Electric having built its original 56-seat body. It is seen in late 1961 at Bradford Moor with its later 63-seat East Lancs body. *(G Lumb)*

Right: Number **675** was numerically the last of the ten rebodied AEC trolleybuses. It is seen unloading at Broadway before turning round into Bank Street to return to Thornbury. This temporary turning circle was constructed in May 1964 and remained in use until the following October. The ten AEC rebodied trolleybuses returned to service in June and July 1956. *(V Nutton courtesy G Lumb Collection)*

Above: The Suez crisis in late 1956 caused oil shortages as vessels were unable to pass through the Suez Canal. As a consequence the Traffic Commissioners required a 10% saving in fuel oil consumption and bus mileage, allowing the former Darlington single-deck trolleybus, **T403**, to be placed in service between the City and Bierley Church. T403 is seen turning at Bierley in July 1957 with a Bankfoot to Bolton Roe-bodied Karrier W4 following. A further six Darlington single-deck Karrier W4 chassis had been purchased in October 1956 for spares. *(J Copland)*

>> Opposite page: Between November 1957 and June 1958 a further twenty trolleybuses returned to service fitted with new East Lancashire Coachbuilders 8ft-wide, 27ft-long bodies; ten of these were Karrier W4 chassis that had previously carried Park Royal Utility bodies. One of them, No. **718**, loads in Tyrrel Street for Wibsey in a street scene bursting with interest. Tyrrel Street was the terminus for Buttershaw services as well as Wibsey and, across the junction, for the Duckworth Lane and Allerton services. *(Roy Brook)*

Above: The other ten of the 20 to be rebodied in 1957/8 comprised the batch of 1941/2 ex-Notts & Derby AEC trolleybuses, 587-96, which were fitted with new East Lancashire 63-seat bodies, 8ft wide and 27ft long, with platform doors. The front axles were modified for the extra width. Number **593** (**HNU 971**) is seen entering Forster Square after descending Church Bank in 1961. *(V Nutton courtesy G Lumb Collection)*

>> *Opposite page:* The bodies on the ten ex-Notts & Derby rebodied AEC trolleybuses were to be the last rear-entrance examples bought new by Bradford. In 1964, when the Inner Ring Road was being built, No. **590** (**HNU 829**) is seen loading at Hall Ings after the wiring had been moved over from Union Street seen in the background. *(Roy Brook)*

<< ***Opposite page:*** Following Darlington's final abandonment of its trolleybus system in July 1957, a further eight Karrier W4 trolleybuses were purchased by Bradford the following August for rebodying as double-deckers. The June 1956 change in the Construction & Use Regulations allowed two-axle vehicles to be built up to 30ft long. At the same time the overall laden weight of vehicles was raised, which allowed many operators, including Bradford, to increase the number of seats in existing vehicles. After withdrawal at the end of January 1958, T403 and these eight chassis from Darlington formed the basis for the next rebuilding exercises; this time allowing Bradford to have new forward-entrance bodies, 28ft 11½ins long (the longest possible on the existing wheelbase), built by East Lancs. These became 785-93 and as built they seated 71. Number **785** (**GHN 403**), which used T403's chassis, is seen at Thornbury in July 1971. *(G Lumb)*

Right: These 71-seat trolleybuses had returned to service between November 1958 and February 1959. The East Lancs bodies were fitted with saloon heaters, an innovation. Number **785** is seen on 29th July 1971, on its way to Clayton and is about to pass under the Pasture Lane railway bridge. This view from above shows how the trolley gear was mounted on the roof. The Clayton route was withdrawn on 31st July. *(G Lumb)*

Above: With further city centre development taking place in 1962, the cross-city service from Bradford Moor to Crossflatts was abandoned to leave trolleybus operation from Forster Square to Crossflatts from a temporary terminus outside the Midland Hotel. This truncated service survived until October 1963. In June 1963 ex-Darlington No. **788** is seen loading among the rubble; in the background are a 1951 BUT and one of the rebodied Darlington BUT trolleybuses. *(Roy Brook)*

>> Opposite page: One of the difficulties in operating these long 71-seat trolleybuses is clearly shown in this view of No. **793** turning at Pasture Lane on 29th July 1971, two days before closure of this route. *(G Lumb)*

Above: After the Darlingtons had been placed in service the works at Thornbury completed the overhaul of eight further second-hand BUT 9611T trolleybuses purchased from St Helens Corporation in 1958. These had been new in 1950/1, with East Lancs 8ft-wide bodies seating 56. After years of neglect at St Helens, Bradford had to carry out extensive repairs to the chassis; the bodies were then refurbished by Charles H Roe at Leeds. The work included replacing corroded metal pillars and reseating to carry 63 passengers. Number **797** is seen loading in Union Street for Tong Cemetery in August 1962. The architect of their decay later followed Humpidge as Bradford's manager. *(G Lumb)*

>> *Opposite page:* The ex-St Helens vehicles entered service between March and July 1959 as Bradford 794-801 (BDJ 82-9). In July 1963 the author photographed No. **798** leaving Union Street for Tong Cemetery, less than ten minutes later the vehicle was parked a half-mile away at the junction of Croft Street and Wakefield Road, with its bodywork damaged. The trolleybus driver hadn't noticed that the jib of a mobile crane stopped at the road junction was projecting into the path of his trolleybus. *(G Lumb)*

and May 1959. The Weymann 56-seat bodies were modified to seat 33 upstairs and 26 down. In May 1959, No. **802** is seen loading in Forster Square for Bradford Moor. The temporary buildings on the site of the YMCA, destroyed by fire in 1950, can be seen in the background. Number 802 was another vehicle to be painted in an experimental livery. *(G Warnes)*

Below: In November 1960, No. **802** was repainted to incorporate more primrose after adverse criticism from the public about the all blue-livery with only one primrose band. On 1st June 1963 the driver attempted to change the destination blinds whilst travelling along Tong Street, with disastrous results. Unrepaired, it was eventually sold for scrap. *(V Nutton courtesy G Lumb Collection)*

<< ***Opposite page:*** One of the trolleybus tours in June 1964 used a former St Helens BUT as the tour vehicle. Number **801** is seen turning at Peel Park on Bolton Road, while one of the buses used to replace cross-city trolleybus route Eccleshill to St Enoch's Road Top is passing. The cross-city service was withdrawn on 17th November 1962; trolleybuses continued to serve Eccleshill until 31st October 1964. The remaining routes using Bolton Road, 40 to Saltaire and 42 to Greengates, were not withdrawn until 30th June 1971, only nine months after the overhead had been replaced using new cadmium-copper wiring, which had been installed by an overhead line crew specially hired from Huddersfield. *(G Warnes)*

Above: In February 1959, two second-hand BUT 9611T trolleybuses were bought from Brighton Corporation. After repainting they entered service as 802/3 (HUF 49/50), in April

Left: Another 1959 purchase, between June and August, was of twelve second-hand Sunbeam W4 trolleybuses from Maidstone and District Motor Services, who had ceased to operate trolleybuses in Hastings at the end of May. One of these, Hastings 21 (**BDY 796**) was identified in chalk as Bradford **806**. It was waiting its turn for overhaul at Thornbury Works in September 1959. Park Royal-bodied, it was new to the Hastings Tramway Company in January 1946. As 806, it entered service in Bradford in July 1960. *(V Nutton courtesy G Lumb Collection)*

>> *Opposite page:* The first ex-Hastings vehicle to enter service was **815** (**BDY 815**), one of two fitted with Weymann 56-seat bodies; like ex-Brighton 802, it was painted in an all-over blue livery with one primrose band when placed into service in August 1959. In this 1960 picture the vehicle, seen entering Union Street on a Dudley Hill short working, had had its upper deck window pillars repainted primrose. Standing alongside is an 8ft-wide version of the same body manufacturer's motorbus body, built new in 1949. *(V Nutton courtesy G Lumb Collection)*

The survival of trolleybuses at Bradford until 1972 would not have been possible without the dedication of the rolling stock engineers and the skilled workforce employed at Thornbury Car Works. Between 1944 and 1963 they refurbished 147 chassis before these were rebodied by contractors. They also overhauled a further 56 second-hand trolleybuses between 1953 and June 1961. All this was done in addition to maintaining the existing fleets of motor- and trolleybuses.

Above: The first of the ten Park Royal-bodied Sunbeams from Hastings to enter service was No. **808** (**BDY 798**) in November 1959. In July 1960, it is seen passing Chester Street bus station used by West Yorkshire, Hebble, Ledgard and some of the Yorkshire Woollen District motorbus services. *(V Nutton courtesy G Lumb Collection)*

>> *Opposite page:* Number **807** (**BDY 797**), one of the ten Park Royal-bodied Sunbeam W4s ex-Maidstone and District, is seen at the Hall Ings terminus of route 89 to Thornbury, which had started on 4th March 1950, when motorbuses replaced the trams on route 9. After reconstruction of the overhead, trolleybuses replaced the buses on 2nd March 1952, and the Thornbury route was linked cross-city to

Thornton on 14th March 1965 as route number 7: peak hour short workings to Spring Head Road were route 6. The 6 ceased to operate in February 1971 and the 7 became Thornton - City, except at morning and evening peak times on weekdays. The architecture of the shelter behind the vehicle was a feature of some of Bradford's city-centre termini, known to local enthusiasts as "Tutankhamen's Tombs". *(G Lumb)*

fit them with new 8ft-wide East Lancashire Coachbuilders forward-entrance bodies, seating 65 or 66. This time, taking advantage of the change in Construction & Use Regulations, the bodies were 27ft 6ins long. These 27 re-entered service between June 1959 and July 1960. Six of them were fitted with trolley retrievers on return to service, a feature visible on No. **713**, one of the 66-seaters, seen leaving Duckworth Lane terminus in 1961. *(V Nutton courtesy G Lumb Collection)*

>> *Opposite page lower left:* In 1959, the Eccleshill (Stony Lane) route 33 was extended to Faltis Square on the Thorpe Edge housing estate. The approach to this terminus was down a 1 in 8 gradient. This half mile extension being opened on 9th August 1959, survived only until 31st October 1964. One of the recently rebodied Karrier W4 trolleybuses, No. **730**, which had returned to service on 11th September, is seen on an enthusiasts' tour at Faltis Square on 13th September 1959. *(Roy Brook)*

Above: In February 1960, Bradford, hungry for spares for its trolley fleet, purchased six BUT 9611T trolleybuses from Doncaster Corporation, who had acquired them from Darlington in 1952. In July 1960, five Karrier type W4 vehicles were purchased from Grimsby-Cleethorpes Transport, and two similar Sunbeam W4 Roe-bodied examples from Ashton-under-Lyne Corporation arrived in September 1960. One of the Ashton Sunbeams, No. **65 (FTJ 401)**, is seen outside the store shed at Thornbury Works, with the recently withdrawn No. **615**, an AEC/EE with NCB Mk II body. *(G Lumb)*

>> *Opposite page upper left:* The arrival of the second-hand Brighton, Hastings and St Helens trolleybuses allowed Bradford to rebuild the 27 remaining utility-bodied Karrier W4 chassis and

>> *Opposite page right:* The roundabout at St Enoch's Road Top is the location of this view on 28th July 1971, when No. **732**, one of the 27 forward entrance DKY-registered trolleybuses to return to service in 1959/60 after rebodying, is returning to the City from Wibsey. The Wibsey and Buttershaw services were withdrawn on 31st July 1971. *(G Lumb)*

<< *Opposite page:* Bradford's next batch of five rebodied trolleybuses entered service in July and August 1961, again having 27ft 6ins-long, forward-entrance, 66 seat (37 upstairs and 29 down) bodies. This time the chassis used were third-hand 1949 BUT 9611Ts, which had seen service in Darlington and Doncaster. These five, LHN 781-5, became 831-5 at Bradford. Number **832** is seen working an enthusiasts' tour in September 1962 at Allerton Road on the City side of Chapel Lane turning circle. These vehicles introduced the deeper windscreen to improve driving visibility. The later photograph (on page 76) shows one of each design. *(G Lumb)*

Right: Number **833**, another of the five rebodied BUT trolleybuses originally from Darlington, is seen on 29th July 1971 turning at Pasture Lane, two days before closure of the Clayton, Wibsey and Buttershaw routes, the biggest closure at any one time. *(G Lumb)*

with the much larger Sheffield undertaking. Before he left on 2nd May 1961, he had purchased twelve Sunbeam F4 chassis from the Mexborough and Swinton system. Orders had been placed for twelve new bodies for the former Ashton and Grimsby chassis. His successor, John C Wake, took office on 3rd July 1961 and changes in policy followed. The electrical equipment from four of the Mexborough Sunbeams was transferred to some of the earlier Darlingtons, 785-8. The body order was reduced to seven, and these were fitted to the refurbished chassis of seven of the Mexborough Sunbeams. These seven were 8ft wide, 28ft 6ins long and seated 66; they entered service between October 1962 and February 1963, as fleet Nos 841-4 (FWX 911-4) and 845-7 (JWW 375-7). Number **842** is seen in Hall Ings, working to Holme Wood, which was the last route extension to be built; opening on 6th March 1960, it lasted only until 1st April 1967, when the Wakefield Road routes were withdrawn. *(Roy Brook)*

Above: June 1971 was the twilight of the Bradford trolleybus, and this busy scene at the bottom of Thornton Road shows rebodied East Lancs (both front- and rear-entrance versions) DKY-registered Karrier trolleybuses. When the remaining Bolton Road routes 40 and 42 were withdrawn on 30th June 1971, all remaining rear entrance vehicles were also withdrawn. *(D J Smithies)*

>> *Opposite page:* In early 1961, Bradford's Manager, C T Humpidge, moved to the same post

Duckworth Lane. Initially using a fleet of 20 forward-entrance trolleybuses, all operating from Duckworth Lane depot, the services had motorbuses substituted for certain duties from 8th November 1971. In January 1972 the City Council decided that the final date for trolleybus operation should be 26th March 1972. Then disaster struck: lack of coal to feed the power stations, because of the miners' strike, caused major power cuts affecting all users.

Above: The difference in length between the 27 DKY-registered rebodied 27ft 6ins machines and the seven Mexborough Sunbeams is shown in this view of Nos **708** and **845** in Thornton Road. Both bodies seated 66 and they had been new in March 1960 and December 1962. The support frames constructed to carry the new bodywork on these forward-entrance vehicles were fractured on 24 of 25 vehicles examined in 1971 at Duckworth Lane depot: the odd one was 706, which was thus selected for preservation. *(Roy Brook)*

>> *Opposite page:* With the closure of three routes on 31st July 1971, Britain was left with just two trolleybus services: Bradford's route 7 linking Thornton and Thornbury, and the 8 from City Centre to Bradford Royal Infirmary on

As a result, trolleybuses were withdrawn from service on 10th February. As power was restored, trolleybuses started returning to service on 7th March and by the 11th, eleven were available for duties. On Saturday 18th March two were in use on route 8 and three on the 7. One of the two Mexboroughs on the 8 was No. **846**, seen at the terminus. *(G Lumb)*

Above: Number **706**, one of the last service trolleybuses to leave Thornbury for Thornton, is seen in the late-afternoon sunshine of Friday, 24th March. On the extreme right of the group of bystanders witnessing this memorable occasion is Jim Copland, photographer extraordinaire, whose work since 1950 has enhanced so many publications dealing with Bradford trolleybuses. Later that evening, at 10.52pm, No. 706 became the last trolleybus to work a scheduled service from the City to Duckworth Lane, and No. 843 was the last trolleybus to work a scheduled trolleybus service anywhere in Great Britain, when it left the City at 10.57pm for Thornton, before returning to Duckworth Lane depot at 11.32pm. *(D J Smithies)*

Number 706 and ten further former Bradford trolleybuses can still be seen at the Trolleybus Museum at Sandtoft, which is situated at a former aerodrome on the Isle of Axholme, North Lincolnshire, between Doncaster and Scunthorpe. Details can be obtained from the Operations Department, Sandtoft Transport Centre Ltd, Sandtoft, Doncaster, South Yorkshire, DN8 5SX, telephone 01724 711391 (24-hour info. line).

On Saturday, 25th March and Sunday morning, 26th March, special tours were operated for enthusiasts by the Transport Department. During Sunday afternoon, the last trolleybus system was ceremonially closed. The Lord Mayor, civic dignitaries and invited guests were transported over the last routes, using trolleybus No. **844**, which had been suitably decorated with both "Britain's" and "Bradford's Last Trolleybus" slogans. This view shows the crowds waiting to see this last trolleybus depart at 3pm. The Lord Mayor, Alderman H Moran, JP, a former trolleybus driver, is seen climbing into the driver's cab to join Mr Frederick Kelly, the longest-serving driver; the Lord Mayor's car, a 4.2-litre Daimler, departmental number **01**, registration **LKY 1G**, prepares to lead the way. Behind 844 is one of the tower wagons, with overhead linesmen in attendance to ensure that nothing went wrong. *(Roy Brook)*

Many hundreds of well-wishers were waiting to greet **844** on its return to Thornbury with the civic party at about 4.30pm on Sunday, 26th March 1972. They were all aware that Britain's last surviving trolleybus system had operated its last vehicle. These spectators were invited into the works to hear the speeches from various dignitaries, before the power was switched off at 5.07pm consigning 61 years of trolleybus operation to history. Our final tribute shows the Manager, Edward Deakin, giving his final speech; behind him, looking upwards, is J Stanley King, Deputy Convenor of the Transport Executive Group, who had for over 30 years vigorously supported the use and development of trolleybuses in Bradford. *(Roy Brook)*